1694

The Lion

King of the Beasts

by Christine and Michel Denis-Huot

ikai **Charlesbridge**

Library of Congress Cataloging-in-Publication Data
Denis-Huot, Christine.
        [Lion, roi fainéant. English]
    The lion, king of the beasts/Christine and Michel Denis-Huot.
        p.   cm.—(Animal close-ups)
    Includes bibliographical references (p.   ).
    Summary: Describes the physical characteristics, behavior, and
habitat of lions and discusses other big cats to which they are
related.
    ISBN 1-57091-426-5 (softcover)
    1. Lions—Juvenile literature. [1. Lions.] I. Denis-Huot, Michel.
II. Title. III. Series.

QL737.C23 D4513 2000
599.757—dc21   99-048027

Copyright © 2000 by Charlesbridge Publishing
Translated by Lisa Laird

Copyright © 1993 by Éditions Milan under the title *le lion, roi fainéant*
300 rue Léon-Joulin, 31101 Toulouse Cedex 100, France
French series editor, Valérie Tracqui

Published by Charlesbridge Publishing, 85 Main Street, Watertown, MA 02472
(617) 926-0329 • www.charlesbridge.com
Printed in Korea
        10 9 8 7 6 5 4 3 2 1

Lazy afternoons

The African savanna stretches as far as the eye can see. In the shadow of an acacia tree, nine lionesses sleep peacefully with their cubs. Gazelles graze calmly nearby. They know that lions are only dangerous when they hide in the tall grass, ready to spring on unsuspecting prey.

The lions have been dozing since morning. They rest most of the day, but as the sun sets, the big cats stretch and yawn. Each lioness cleans and brushes herself with her raspy tongue.

The lion can live in any habitat as long as there is enough water, but it prefers grassy savannas that offer plenty of places to hide.

Resting in plain sight, this lion is not a danger to nearby prey.

Big prides often separate into smaller groups scattered across the pride's territory.

Lions love to play together.

The lion's roar can be heard for many miles over flat land.

A strong sisterhood

These lionesses are all from the same family. Mothers, daughters, sisters, and cousins are all equal in the lion community, called a pride. Two adult males lead the group, but they are not related to any of the females. Males only stay with the pride for a few years. Females spend their whole lives together.

Night falls, and the lions begin to roar. Each male fills his chest with air and lowers his head toward the ground. A deep rumble explodes into a full-throated roar, and the earth vibrates with sound. The lionesses growl softly in response.

Whenever lionesses of the same pride meet, they touch and rub each other to say hello.

7

Private property

The lion's roar warns trespassers to stay away. Although two or three males often lead a pride together, they fiercely chase away any strange males they meet.

The lion patrols its territory every day, stopping regularly to mark the area with urine and scent. The smell becomes an invisible fence that makes other lions turn away.

Sometimes young lions without a pride of their own dare to challenge a pride's leaders. Lions can be badly hurt in these battles, and some may even be killed. The winners force the losers to leave the territory and live on their own.

The lion's mane is its most distinctive feature. The color can vary from pale yellow to black.

The lion claws the ground to help mark its territory.

New lion chiefs may kill the cubs fathered by the defeated lions so that the pride's lionesses will be ready to mate sooner.

Males fight frequently and are often covered in scars.

Mating lions stay together for several days. They do not eat during this time, and they ignore prey that passes in front of them.

Mating only lasts a few seconds at a time, but lions will mate thirty to forty times a day.

Tough love

When a lioness is ready to mate, one of the males leads her away from the rest of the pride. She follows, but she does not accept his advances right away. The male may spend a few hours chasing her before the lioness finally allows him to approach.

Both lions growl and bare their teeth while they mate. The mating may look violent, but the lions never hurt each other and soon quiet down. They doze peacefully together for a short time before beginning the game all over again.

The lioness may chase her mate away immediately after mating, but she quickly allows him to come back.

Cuddly cubs

Three months later, the lioness leaves the pride and looks for a safe place where she can give birth. Before long, she is surrounded by up to six tiny cubs, begging for milk.

The cubs begin to walk when they are about three weeks old, but they must not wander far. It is easy to get lost in the high grass, and leopards and hyenas might catch and kill them.

When the cubs are almost two months old, their mother introduces them to the pride. At first she bares her teeth at every lion that comes near, but the new family quickly adjusts to group life.

A baby lion weighs only four pounds at birth. Its fur is spotted, and its eyes are closed. A cub usually opens its eyes when it is about a week old.

Everything is an excuse to play for a young lion cub.

The lioness may move her family to a new hiding place every three or four days.

Lunchtime is over, but the lioness sometimes has to growl and pull herself away from her greedy cubs.

If their mother dies, the cubs will be adopted by another lioness in the pride.

One big family

Lion cubs play together in a big group as soon as they join the pride. They play-fight, chase, and cuddle. It is hard to tell which cubs belong to each mother.

When the cubs get hungry, they find a lioness willing to feed them. Any mother in the pride will do. Sometimes a lioness is surrounded by as many as ten hungry cubs, all looking for milk.

When the lionesses go hunting, one of them stays behind to look after all the cubs. The babysitter may not even have cubs of her own. Every member of the pride helps to raise the young.

The hunt

Night falls, and it is time to hunt. A herd of impalas does not see the lionesses slowly circling around it. Suddenly one lioness attacks, driving the impalas straight toward the other hunters.

The waiting lionesses spring forward and quickly pull down the weakest impala. Hunting in a group makes catching big game much easier.

Lions must count on surprising the animals they hunt because most of their prey can run faster than they can. Even with a large group of hunters, only about one-quarter of the hunts end with a kill.

Lionesses sometimes hunt during the day, but they have excellent night vision and prefer to hunt at night when they can hide in the darkness.

Lions do not chase an animal for very long. If they cannot catch it within the first few yards, the hunt is a failure.

The lion's share

The two male lions watch the hunt from a distance. They rarely hunt for themselves, relying on the lionesses to kill for them. The huntresses quickly swallow as much meat as they can. The male lions will soon chase them away. It is the law of the jungle: the strongest takes what it can.

The lion eats many different animals, including gnu, zebras, gazelles, buffalo, and sometimes even giraffes or young hippopotamuses.

The lion also eats carrion, but it often has to scare away vultures and hyenas that want a share of the carcass.

Always on the lookout for a meal, a vulture circles above the lion kill. It will feed on the scraps the lions leave behind.

The lionesses return to feed once the males have eaten their fill. Before long, there is nothing left of the impala. The big cats have eaten enough meat for five days in just one meal. They stuff themselves because they know that they will not get to eat every day.

Once fed, the lion drinks from a water hole, then stretches out to relax and digest its meal.

Hungry cubs

Young cubs begin eating bits of meat when they are three months old. They love to play with the bones after a kill. But older cubs often chase the younger ones away from the few scraps that are left.

Adult lions eat before the cubs even when prey is rare. The young often have to do without, and many die from starvation.

The most cunning cubs survive by getting milk from one of the lionesses long after the cub is too old for it. This often means the lioness's own babies will go hungry.

The bigger the pride, the better chance a cub has to reach adulthood.

A lion cub must learn to hunt. At first it can catch only small animals.

Cubs often play-fight to test their strength and agility.

Even a majestic lion sometimes plays with the pride's cubs.

Exile

When they are three years old, male cubs are expelled from the pride's territory so that they cannot challenge the pride's leaders. The young lions now have to hunt and protect themselves from enemies.

One day, the young lions will fight to take over a pride. If they win, they will force the pride's defeated leaders to leave the territory and live alone.

Meanwhile, female cubs stay in the territory where they were born. If all goes well, they will have cubs every two years. Even when they are too old to hunt and care for cubs, they will be protected by the other lionesses in the pride.

Only groups of two or three males working together can maintain control of a pride for many years.

Confined to reserves

The lion's territory is shrinking rapidly as more roads and farms take over the land. Game reserves offer a place where the lion can live comfortably, disturbed only by tourists' cameras.

Scientists can tell lions apart by the pattern of their whiskers.

Shrinking habitat

The lion once lived all over Africa, Europe, Central Asia, and even Alaska. But the big cats began to disappear thousands of years ago. The last European lions lived in Greece in the first century. Except for a small population in the Gir Forest of India, the lion now lives only in Africa.

Sadly, the king of the beasts is still not safe. Trophy hunters and farmers protecting their livestock kill many lions. Expanding agriculture continues to take over their territory. Fewer and fewer lions now live outside the protected game reserves.

These lions are accustomed to tourists.

Reserve life

Tourists do not seem to bother the reserve lions, and the cats often let cars come quite close. Because the lion hunts at night, tourism rarely disrupts a hunt, and the lion can live quite comfortably. However, conservationists cannot allow reserve prides to grow too big, or they will tip the delicate balance between predator and prey.

Research

The lion fascinates scientists because it is the only species of wild cat that lives in a social group. Researchers have been studying the behavior of lions in the Serengeti since 1963. Each lion has an identity card showing pictures of its whiskers and other identifying marks so that scientists will know which lion they are observing.

Some lions wear radio collars that send a signal for three years, allowing scientists to study the lions' movements.

Lion attacks

The lion is afraid of humans and kills only under exceptional circumstances. It becomes a man-eater only if it is too old or sick to catch other prey. Because the whole pride cares for its members, a weak lion that belongs to a pride does not have to attack humans to survive.

More wild cats

The lion is a carnivore with sharp teeth and retractable claws like a house cat. It is the only species of large cat that lives with others of its kind. Most wild cats prefer to live alone.

▲ The tiger is the biggest and heaviest o the wild cats. It can be found from India to Siberia and also in China. The tiger has a fierce reputation as a man-eater, and it has been hunted almost to extinction everywhere except in India.

◄ The leopard lives in Africa, Asia, and the Middle East. It climbs trees easily and often drags its prey high into the branches where other predators cannot reach it. Some people call leopards *panthers*, particularly the ones born with solid black fur. In some parts of the world, other wild cats are also called panthers. The Florida panther, for example, is actually a subspecies of the cougar, a North America wild cat.

The snow leopard cannot roar, but it can purr like a house cat. Its fur varies from creamy white to gray. The snow leopard is very well adapted to its home in the cold mountains of central Asia. It has very thick fur and big paws for walking in the snow. The snow leopard is now one of the rarest species of wild cat. Few people have ever seen one outside a zoo.

◄ The jaguar looks a lot like a leopard, but it is much bigger. It lives only in South and Central America, making its home in rain forests, grasslands, and even in rocky areas. Like other big cats, it suffers from having beautiful fur and is now very rare.

For Further Reading on Lions . . .

Arnold, Caroline. <u>Lion</u>. Morrow, 1995.

Fowler, Allan. <u>Really Big Cats</u>. Children's Press, 1998.

Harman, Amanda. <u>Lions</u>. Benchmark, 1997.

To See Lions in Captivity . . .

Folzenlogen, Darcy and Robert. <u>The Guide to American Zoos and Aquariums</u>. Willow Press, 1993.

Many zoos also have Web sites on the Internet. To learn more about their exhibits, go to the following page on the Yahoo WWW site:

http://dir.yahoo.com/Science/Biology/Zoology/Zoos

Use the Internet to Find Out More about Lions and Other Wild Cats. . . .

Africam
—Read about lion breeding and behavior, then peek through a live camera to see wildlife gather at water holes in South Africa's game reserves!
http://africam.com

Lion Research Center
—Hear a lion roar, learn to identify individual lions, meet the lions of the Serengeti, and find out how you can help scientists learn more about lions.
http://www.lionresearch.org

Rolling Hills Refuge Wildlife Conservation Center: African Lion
—See detailed information about lions and conservation efforts, read fun facts, and take a test to show how much you have learned.
http://rhrwildlife.com/lionadv.htm

See Updated Animal Close-Ups Internet Resources. . . .
http://www.charlesbridge.com

Photograph Credits:

Bios/WWF: Rey Millet, p. 27 (bottom); C. and M. Denis-Huot: all other photographs.